TODAY
I MANIFEST & CREATE THE LIFE I DESIRE

This 369 Manifestation Workbook Belongs to:

Copyright © 2021 369 Method: The Law of Attraction Writing Exercise Journal & Workbook to Manifest Your Desires with the 3-6-9 Manifestation Technique

All rights reserved. No part of this book may be reproduced in any form or by any electronic or mechanical means, including information storage and retrieval systems, without permission in writing from the publisher, except by reviewers, who may quote brief passages in a review.

Make it Happen Publishing Inc.

www.mihpublishing.com
Send all inquires to books@mihpublishing.com

THE LAW OF ATTRACTION TECHNIQUE: 3-6-9 Method

WHAT TO DO:

Focus on one goal and write out a clear statement in the present tense (like you already have it and from a place of gratitude) that outlines what you desire in 17 seconds (approx. the three lines provided). Write out the statement 3 times in the morning, 6 times in the afternoon and 9 times in the evening for up to 45 days - it may manifest earlier - in that case express gratitude and begin a new intention!

(For example: "I am excited, overjoyed and grateful for the extra $10,000 in my bank account this month")

3-6-9 MANIFESTATION TIPS

- Remove any possible distractions and be mindful and present when writing your lines.

- Be clear and detailed about what you want to manifest. It should take 17 seconds to write.

- Including words of gratitude and emotions into your statement are essential!

- Be excited about what you are manifesting - Feel the emotions of receiving what you want.

- Come up with a statement that resonates with you and your desire.

- Try to do the morning, afternoon and evening writing around the same time everyday.

- This is not homework and it should not feel bad to do. Get into a high vibrational space.

- Saying the words as you write them can help keep you focused.

- Visualize your life as you want it to be and meditating before & after is beneficial.

- At the end of 45 days (or the duration that resonates with your desire) release your desire or affirmation and trust that the Universe will bring it to you.

- When you've completed the 369 challenge and have successfully manifested your goal, remember to record your success in this journal for future reference and confirmation.

- Finally don't forget to show gratitude and express it with authenticity!

>> Optional Variation: In the morning, INITIATE your manifestation by writing one name, word, object or short affirmation about your desire 3 times. In the afternoon AMPLIFY and expand it with your intention for what you wrote in the morning. In the evening COMPLETE your manifestation with what your final goal or desired action is using words of gratitude and the emotions and feelings associated with the outcome - this final statement should be 17 seconds in length.

>> Duration: 21 days, 30 days, 33 days or 45 days - choose the length that resonates with you.

*** *NOW GO AND GET STARTED ON MANIFESTING THE LIFE YOU WANT AND DESERVE!* ***

DATE ____/____/____ **369 METHOD - DAY** 1 of ☐

MORNING AFFIRMATION (INITIATE) TIME ____:____ AM

1

2

3

AFTERNOON INTENTION (AMPLIFY) TIME ____:____ PM

1

2

3

4

5

6

369 METHOD - DAY 1 of ☐

EVENING GOAL/DESIRED ACTION (COMPLETE)   TIME ____:____ PM

1.
2.
3.
4.
5.
6.
7.
8.
9.

I RELEASE MY INTENTION WITH GRATITUDE AND LOVE,

DATE ____/____/____

369 METHOD - DAY ☐ of ☐

MORNING AFFIRMATION (INITIATE)   TIME ____:____ AM

1

2

3

AFTERNOON INTENTION (AMPLIFY)   TIME ____:____ PM

1

2

3

4

5

6

369 METHOD - DAY ☐ of ☐

EVENING GOAL/DESIRED ACTION (COMPLETE)　　　　TIME ____:____ PM

1.

2.

3.

4.

5.

6.

7.

8.

9.

I RELEASE MY INTENTION WITH GRATITUDE AND LOVE,

DATE ____/____/____   **369 METHOD - DAY** ☐ of ☐

MORNING AFFIRMATION (INITIATE)   TIME ____:____ AM

1

2

3

AFTERNOON INTENTION (AMPLIFY)   TIME ____:____ PM

1

2

3

4

5

6

369 METHOD - DAY ☐ of ☐

EVENING GOAL/DESIRED ACTION (COMPLETE)　　　　TIME ____:____ PM

1

2

3

4

5

6

7

8

9

I RELEASE MY INTENTION WITH GRATITUDE AND LOVE,

DATE ____/____/____   **369 METHOD - DAY ☐ of ☐**

MORNING AFFIRMATION (INITIATE)   TIME ____:____ AM

1

2

3

AFTERNOON INTENTION (AMPLIFY)   TIME ____:____ PM

1

2

3

4

5

6

369 METHOD - DAY ☐ of ☐

EVENING GOAL/DESIRED ACTION (COMPLETE)　　　TIME ____:____ PM

1

2

3

4

5

6

7

8

9

I RELEASE MY INTENTION WITH GRATITUDE AND LOVE,

DATE ____/____/____ **369 METHOD - DAY** ☐ of ☐

MORNING AFFIRMATION (INITIATE)   TIME ____:____ AM

1

2

3

AFTERNOON INTENTION (AMPLIFY)   TIME ____:____ PM

1

2

3

4

5

6

369 METHOD - DAY ☐ of ☐

EVENING GOAL/DESIRED ACTION (COMPLETE)   TIME ____:____ PM

1

2

3

4

5

6

7

8

9

I RELEASE MY INTENTION WITH GRATITUDE AND LOVE,

DATE ____/____/____

369 METHOD - DAY ☐ of ☐

MORNING AFFIRMATION (INITIATE)　　　　　　　　　　　TIME ____:____ AM

1

2

3

AFTERNOON INTENTION (AMPLIFY)　　　　　　　　　　TIME ____:____ PM

1

2

3

4

5

6

369 METHOD - DAY ☐ of ☐

EVENING GOAL/DESIRED ACTION (COMPLETE)　　　TIME ____:____ PM

1.

2.

3.

4.

5.

6.

7.

8.

9.

I RELEASE MY INTENTION WITH GRATITUDE AND LOVE,

DATE ____/____/____　　　　　　　　　　**369 METHOD - DAY** ☐ of ☐

MORNING AFFIRMATION (INITIATE)　　　　　TIME ____:____ AM

1

2

3

AFTERNOON INTENTION (AMPLIFY)　　　　　TIME ____:____ PM

1

2

3

4

5

6

369 METHOD - DAY ☐ of ☐

EVENING GOAL/DESIRED ACTION (COMPLETE)   TIME ____:____ PM

1.

2.

3.

4.

5.

6.

7.

8.

9.

I RELEASE MY INTENTION WITH GRATITUDE AND LOVE,

DATE ___/___/___   **369 METHOD - DAY** ☐ of ☐

MORNING AFFIRMATION (INITIATE)   TIME ___:___ AM

1

2

3

AFTERNOON INTENTION (AMPLIFY)   TIME ___:___ PM

1

2

3

4

5

6

369 METHOD - DAY ☐ of ☐

EVENING GOAL/DESIRED ACTION (COMPLETE) TIME ____:____ PM

1

2

3

4

5

6

7

8

9

I RELEASE MY INTENTION WITH GRATITUDE AND LOVE,

DATE ____/____/____ **369 METHOD - DAY** ☐ of ☐

MORNING AFFIRMATION (INITIATE) TIME ____:____ AM

1

2

3

AFTERNOON INTENTION (AMPLIFY) TIME ____:____ PM

1

2

3

4

5

6

MORNING AFFIRMATION (INITIATE)

369 METHOD - DAY ☐ of ☐

EVENING GOAL/DESIRED ACTION (COMPLETE)   TIME ____:____ PM

1

2

3

4

5

6

7

8

9

I RELEASE MY INTENTION WITH GRATITUDE AND LOVE,

DATE ____/____/____   **369 METHOD - DAY** ☐ of ☐

MORNING AFFIRMATION (INITIATE)   TIME ____:____ AM

1

2

3

AFTERNOON INTENTION (AMPLIFY)   TIME ____:____ PM

1

2

3

4

5

6

369 METHOD - DAY ☐ of ☐

EVENING GOAL/DESIRED ACTION (COMPLETE)　　　TIME ____:____ PM

1

2

3

4

5

6

7

8

9

I RELEASE MY INTENTION WITH GRATITUDE AND LOVE,

DATE ____/____/____ **369 METHOD - DAY** ☐ of ☐

MORNING AFFIRMATION (INITIATE)   TIME ____:____ AM

1

2

3

AFTERNOON INTENTION (AMPLIFY)   TIME ____:____ PM

1

2

3

4

5

6

369 METHOD - DAY ☐ of ☐

EVENING GOAL/DESIRED ACTION (COMPLETE)   TIME ____:____ PM

1

2

3

4

5

6

7

8

9

I RELEASE MY INTENTION WITH GRATITUDE AND LOVE,

DATE ____/____/____ **369 METHOD - DAY** ☐ of ☐

MORNING AFFIRMATION (INITIATE)   TIME ____:____ AM

1

2

3

AFTERNOON INTENTION (AMPLIFY)   TIME ____:____ PM

1

2

3

4

5

6

1

369 METHOD - DAY ☐ of ☐

EVENING GOAL/DESIRED ACTION (COMPLETE) TIME ____:____ PM

1

2

3

4

5

6

7

8

9

I RELEASE MY INTENTION WITH GRATITUDE AND LOVE,

DATE ____/____/____

369 METHOD - DAY ☐ of ☐

MORNING AFFIRMATION (INITIATE)   TIME ____:____ AM

1

2

3

AFTERNOON INTENTION (AMPLIFY)   TIME ____:____ PM

1

2

3

4

5

6

369 METHOD - DAY ☐ of ☐

EVENING GOAL/DESIRED ACTION (COMPLETE) TIME ____:____ PM

1
2
3
4
5
6
7
8
9

I RELEASE MY INTENTION WITH GRATITUDE AND LOVE,

DATE ____/____/____   **369 METHOD - DAY** ☐ of ☐

MORNING AFFIRMATION (INITIATE)   TIME ____:____ AM

1

2

3

AFTERNOON INTENTION (AMPLIFY)   TIME ____:____ PM

1

2

3

4

5

6

369 METHOD - DAY ☐ of ☐

EVENING GOAL/DESIRED ACTION (COMPLETE)　　　TIME ____:____ PM

1

2

3

4

5

6

7

8

9

I RELEASE MY INTENTION WITH GRATITUDE AND LOVE,

DATE ____/____/____

369 METHOD - DAY ☐ of ☐

MORNING AFFIRMATION (INITIATE)   TIME ____:____ AM

1

2

3

AFTERNOON INTENTION (AMPLIFY)   TIME ____:____ PM

1

2

3

4

5

6

369 METHOD - DAY ☐ of ☐

EVENING GOAL/DESIRED ACTION (COMPLETE)   TIME ____:____ PM

1

2

3

4

5

6

7

8

9

I RELEASE MY INTENTION WITH GRATITUDE AND LOVE,

DATE ____/____/____   **369 METHOD - DAY** ☐ of ☐

MORNING AFFIRMATION (INITIATE) TIME ____:____ AM

1

2

3

AFTERNOON INTENTION (AMPLIFY) TIME ____:____ PM

1

2

3

4

5

6

369 METHOD - DAY ☐ of ☐

EVENING GOAL/DESIRED ACTION (COMPLETE) TIME ____:____ PM

1

2

3

4

5

6

7

8

9

I RELEASE MY INTENTION WITH GRATITUDE AND LOVE,

DATE ____/____/____

369 METHOD - DAY ☐ of ☐

MORNING AFFIRMATION (INITIATE)   TIME ____:____ AM

1
2
3

AFTERNOON INTENTION (AMPLIFY)   TIME ____:____ PM

1
2
3
4
5
6

369 METHOD - DAY ☐ of ☐

EVENING GOAL/DESIRED ACTION (COMPLETE) TIME ____:____ PM

1.

2.

3.

4.

5.

6.

7.

8.

9.

I RELEASE MY INTENTION WITH GRATITUDE AND LOVE,

DATE ____/____/____

369 METHOD - DAY ☐ *of* ☐

MORNING AFFIRMATION (INITIATE)   TIME ____:____ AM

1

2

3

AFTERNOON INTENTION (AMPLIFY)   TIME ____:____ PM

1

2

3

4

5

6

369 METHOD - DAY ☐ of ☐

EVENING GOAL/DESIRED ACTION (COMPLETE) TIME ____:____ PM

1. _____

2. _____

3. _____

4. _____

5. _____

6. _____

7. _____

8. _____

9. _____

I RELEASE MY INTENTION WITH GRATITUDE AND LOVE,

DATE ____/____/____

369 METHOD - DAY ☐ of ☐

MORNING AFFIRMATION (INITIATE)

TIME ____:____ AM

1

2

3

AFTERNOON INTENTION (AMPLIFY)

TIME ____:____ PM

1

2

3

4

5

6

369 METHOD - DAY ☐ of ☐

EVENING GOAL/DESIRED ACTION (COMPLETE) TIME ____:____ PM

1.

2.

3.

4.

5.

6.

7.

8.

9.

I RELEASE MY INTENTION WITH GRATITUDE AND LOVE,

DATE ____/____/____

369 METHOD - DAY ☐ of ☐

MORNING AFFIRMATION (INITIATE)

TIME ____:____ AM

1

2

3

AFTERNOON INTENTION (AMPLIFY)

TIME ____:____ PM

1

2

3

4

5

6

369 METHOD - DAY ☐ of ☐

EVENING GOAL/DESIRED ACTION (COMPLETE)   TIME ____:____ PM

1.

2.

3.

4.

5.

6.

7.

8.

9.

I RELEASE MY INTENTION WITH GRATITUDE AND LOVE,

DATE ____/____/____ **369 METHOD - DAY** ☐ of ☐

MORNING AFFIRMATION (INITIATE) TIME ____:____ AM

1

2

3

AFTERNOON INTENTION (AMPLIFY) TIME ____:____ PM

1

2

3

4

5

6

369 METHOD - DAY ☐ of ☐

EVENING GOAL/DESIRED ACTION (COMPLETE) TIME ____:____ PM

1.
2.
3.
4.
5.
6.
7.
8.
9.

I RELEASE MY INTENTION WITH GRATITUDE AND LOVE,

DATE ____/____/____   **369 METHOD - DAY** ☐ of ☐

MORNING AFFIRMATION (INITIATE)   TIME ____:____ AM

1

2

3

AFTERNOON INTENTION (AMPLIFY)   TIME ____:____ PM

1

2

3

4

5

6

369 METHOD - DAY ☐ of ☐

EVENING GOAL/DESIRED ACTION (COMPLETE)   TIME ____:____ PM

1.

2.

3.

4.

5.

6.

7.

8.

9.

I RELEASE MY INTENTION WITH GRATITUDE AND LOVE,

DATE ____/____/____   **369 METHOD - DAY** ☐ of ☐

MORNING AFFIRMATION (INITIATE)   TIME ____:____ AM

1

2

3

AFTERNOON INTENTION (AMPLIFY)   TIME ____:____ PM

1

2

3

4

5

6

369 METHOD - DAY ☐ of ☐

EVENING GOAL/DESIRED ACTION (COMPLETE)   TIME ____:____ PM

1

2

3

4

5

6

7

8

9

I RELEASE MY INTENTION WITH GRATITUDE AND LOVE,

DATE ____/____/____   **369 METHOD - DAY** ☐ of ☐

MORNING AFFIRMATION (INITIATE)   TIME ____:____ AM

1

2

3

AFTERNOON INTENTION (AMPLIFY)   TIME ____:____ PM

1

2

3

4

5

6

369 METHOD - DAY ☐ of ☐

EVENING GOAL/DESIRED ACTION (COMPLETE)　　　　TIME ____:____ PM

1

2

3

4

5

6

7

8

9

I RELEASE MY INTENTION WITH GRATITUDE AND LOVE,

DATE ____/____/____ **369 METHOD - DAY** ☐ of ☐

MORNING AFFIRMATION (INITIATE) TIME ____:____ AM

1
2
3

AFTERNOON INTENTION (AMPLIFY) TIME ____:____ PM

1
2
3
4
5
6

369 METHOD - DAY ☐ of ☐

EVENING GOAL/DESIRED ACTION (COMPLETE)   TIME _____:_____ PM

1

2

3

4

5

6

7

8

9

I RELEASE MY INTENTION WITH GRATITUDE AND LOVE,

DATE ____/____/____

369 METHOD - DAY ☐ of ☐

MORNING AFFIRMATION (INITIATE)   TIME ____:____ AM

1

2

3

AFTERNOON INTENTION (AMPLIFY)   TIME ____:____ PM

1

2

3

4

5

6

369 METHOD - DAY ☐ of ☐

EVENING GOAL/DESIRED ACTION (COMPLETE)   TIME ____:____ PM

1.

2.

3.

4.

5.

6.

7.

8.

9.

I RELEASE MY INTENTION WITH GRATITUDE AND LOVE,

DATE ____/____/____   **369 METHOD - DAY** ☐ of ☐

MORNING AFFIRMATION (INITIATE)   TIME ____:____ AM

1

2

3

AFTERNOON INTENTION (AMPLIFY)   TIME ____:____ PM

1

2

3

4

5

6

369 METHOD - DAY ☐ of ☐

EVENING GOAL/DESIRED ACTION (COMPLETE)   TIME ____:____ PM

1

2

3

4

5

6

7

8

9

I RELEASE MY INTENTION WITH GRATITUDE AND LOVE,

DATE ____/____/____ **369 METHOD - DAY** ☐ of ☐

MORNING AFFIRMATION (INITIATE) TIME ____:____ AM

1

2

3

AFTERNOON INTENTION (AMPLIFY) TIME ____:____ PM

1

2

3

4

5

6

369 METHOD - DAY ☐ of ☐

EVENING GOAL/DESIRED ACTION (COMPLETE)   TIME ____:____ PM

1.

2.

3.

4.

5.

6.

7.

8.

9.

I RELEASE MY INTENTION WITH GRATITUDE AND LOVE,

DATE ____/____/____

369 METHOD - DAY ☐ of ☐

MORNING AFFIRMATION (INITIATE)   TIME ____:____ AM

1
_____
_____
_____

2
_____
_____
_____

3
_____
_____
_____

AFTERNOON INTENTION (AMPLIFY)   TIME ____:____ PM

1
_____
_____
_____

2
_____
_____
_____

3
_____
_____
_____

4
_____
_____
_____

5
_____
_____
_____

6
_____
_____

369 METHOD - DAY ☐ of ☐

EVENING GOAL/DESIRED ACTION (COMPLETE)　　　TIME ____:____ PM

1

2

3

4

5

6

7

8

9

I RELEASE MY INTENTION WITH GRATITUDE AND LOVE,

DATE ____/____/____ **369 METHOD - DAY** ☐ of ☐

MORNING AFFIRMATION (INITIATE) TIME ____:____ AM

1 _____
_____
_____

2 _____
_____
_____

3 _____
_____
_____

AFTERNOON INTENTION (AMPLIFY) TIME ____:____ PM

1 _____
_____
_____

2 _____
_____
_____

3 _____
_____
_____

4 _____
_____
_____

5 _____
_____
_____

6 _____
_____
_____

369 METHOD - DAY ☐ of ☐

EVENING GOAL/DESIRED ACTION (COMPLETE) TIME ____:____ PM

1

2

3

4

5

6

7

8

9

I RELEASE MY INTENTION WITH GRATITUDE AND LOVE,

DATE ____/____/____   **369 METHOD - DAY** ☐ *of* ☐

MORNING AFFIRMATION (INITIATE)   TIME ____:____ AM

1

2

3

AFTERNOON INTENTION (AMPLIFY)   TIME ____:____ PM

1

2

3

4

5

6

MORNING AFFIRMATION (INITIATE)   TIME ____:____ AM

369 METHOD - DAY ☐ of ☐

EVENING GOAL/DESIRED ACTION (COMPLETE)   TIME ____:____ PM

1.

2.

3.

4.

5.

6.

7.

8.

9.

I RELEASE MY INTENTION WITH GRATITUDE AND LOVE,

DATE ____/____/____　　　　　　　　　**369 METHOD -** **DAY** ☐ of ☐

MORNING AFFIRMATION (INITIATE)　　　　　TIME ____:____ AM

1
_____
_____

2
_____
_____

3
_____
_____

AFTERNOON INTENTION (AMPLIFY)　　　　　TIME ____:____ PM

1
_____
_____

2
_____
_____

3
_____
_____

4
_____
_____

5
_____
_____

6
_____
_____

369 METHOD - DAY ☐ of ☐

EVENING GOAL/DESIRED ACTION (COMPLETE)   TIME ____:____ PM

1

2

3

4

5

6

7

8

9

I RELEASE MY INTENTION WITH GRATITUDE AND LOVE,

DATE ____/____/____ **369 METHOD - DAY** ☐ of ☐

MORNING AFFIRMATION (INITIATE)   TIME ____:____ AM

1.

2.

3.

AFTERNOON INTENTION (AMPLIFY)   TIME ____:____ PM

1.

2.

3.

4.

5.

6.

369 METHOD - DAY ☐ of ☐

EVENING GOAL/DESIRED ACTION (COMPLETE)   TIME ____:____ PM

1

2

3

4

5

6

7

8

9

I RELEASE MY INTENTION WITH GRATITUDE AND LOVE,

DATE ____/____/____   **369 METHOD - DAY** ☐ of ☐

MORNING AFFIRMATION (INITIATE)   TIME ____:____ AM

1

2

3

AFTERNOON INTENTION (AMPLIFY)   TIME ____:____ PM

1

2

3

4

5

6

369 METHOD - DAY ☐ of ☐

EVENING GOAL/DESIRED ACTION (COMPLETE)   TIME _____:_____ PM

1

2

3

4

5

6

7

8

9

I RELEASE MY INTENTION WITH GRATITUDE AND LOVE,

DATE ____/____/____ **369 METHOD - DAY** ☐ of ☐

MORNING AFFIRMATION (INITIATE)   TIME ____:____ AM

1
_____
_____
_____

2
_____
_____
_____

3
_____
_____
_____

AFTERNOON INTENTION (AMPLIFY)   TIME ____:____ PM

1
_____
_____
_____

2
_____
_____
_____

3
_____
_____
_____

4
_____
_____
_____

5
_____
_____
_____

6
_____
_____
_____

369 METHOD - DAY ☐ of ☐

EVENING GOAL/DESIRED ACTION (COMPLETE)   TIME ____:____ PM

1.

2.

3.

4.

5.

6.

7.

8.

9.

I RELEASE MY INTENTION WITH GRATITUDE AND LOVE,

DATE ____/____/____   **369 METHOD - DAY** ☐ of ☐

MORNING AFFIRMATION (INITIATE)   TIME ____:____ AM

1 _____

2 _____

3 _____

AFTERNOON INTENTION (AMPLIFY)   TIME ____:____ PM

1 _____

2 _____

3 _____

4 _____

5 _____

6 _____

369 METHOD - DAY ☐ of ☐

EVENING GOAL/DESIRED ACTION (COMPLETE)　　　　TIME ____:____ PM

1.

2.

3.

4.

5.

6.

7.

8.

9.

I RELEASE MY INTENTION WITH GRATITUDE AND LOVE,

DATE ____/____/____ **369 METHOD - DAY** ☐ of ☐

MORNING AFFIRMATION (INITIATE) TIME ____:____ AM

1 _____

2 _____

3 _____

AFTERNOON INTENTION (AMPLIFY) TIME ____:____ PM

1 _____

2 _____

3 _____

4 _____

5 _____

6 _____

369 METHOD - DAY ☐ of ☐

EVENING GOAL/DESIRED ACTION (COMPLETE)   TIME ____:____ PM

1.

2.

3.

4.

5.

6.

7.

8.

9.

I RELEASE MY INTENTION WITH GRATITUDE AND LOVE,

DATE ____/____/____ **369 METHOD - DAY** ☐ of ☐

MORNING AFFIRMATION (INITIATE)   TIME ____:____ AM

1

2

3

AFTERNOON INTENTION (AMPLIFY)   TIME ____:____ PM

1

2

3

4

5

6

369 METHOD - DAY ☐ of ☐

EVENING GOAL/DESIRED ACTION (COMPLETE)　　　TIME ____:____ PM

1

2

3

4

5

6

7

8

9

I RELEASE MY INTENTION WITH GRATITUDE AND LOVE,

DATE ____/____/____   **369 METHOD - DAY** ☐ of ☐

MORNING AFFIRMATION (INITIATE)   TIME ____:____ AM

1

2

3

AFTERNOON INTENTION (AMPLIFY)   TIME ____:____ PM

1

2

3

4

5

6

369 METHOD - DAY ☐ of ☐

EVENING GOAL/DESIRED ACTION (COMPLETE)   TIME ____:____ PM

1.

2.

3.

4.

5.

6.

7.

8.

9.

I RELEASE MY INTENTION WITH GRATITUDE AND LOVE,

DATE ____/____/____   **369 METHOD - DAY** ☐ of ☐

MORNING AFFIRMATION (INITIATE)   TIME ____:____ AM

1
_____
_____
_____

2
_____
_____
_____

3
_____
_____
_____

AFTERNOON INTENTION (AMPLIFY)   TIME ____:____ PM

1
_____
_____
_____

2
_____
_____
_____

3
_____
_____
_____

4
_____
_____
_____

5
_____
_____
_____

6
_____
_____

369 METHOD - DAY ☐ of ☐

EVENING GOAL/DESIRED ACTION (COMPLETE)   TIME ____:____ PM

1

2

3

4

5

6

7

8

9

I RELEASE MY INTENTION WITH GRATITUDE AND LOVE,

DATE ____/____/____

369 METHOD - DAY ☐ of ☐

MORNING AFFIRMATION (INITIATE)

TIME ____:____ AM

1

2

3

AFTERNOON INTENTION (AMPLIFY)

TIME ____:____ PM

1

2

3

4

5

6

369 METHOD - DAY ☐ of ☐

EVENING GOAL/DESIRED ACTION (COMPLETE)   TIME ____:____ PM

1.

2.

3.

4.

5.

6.

7.

8.

9.

I RELEASE MY INTENTION WITH GRATITUDE AND LOVE,

DATE ____/____/____ **369 METHOD - DAY** ☐ of ☐

MORNING AFFIRMATION (INITIATE)　　　　　　　　　　TIME ____:____ AM

1
_____
_____
_____

2
_____
_____
_____

3
_____
_____
_____

AFTERNOON INTENTION (AMPLIFY)　　　　　　　　　　TIME ____:____ PM

1
_____
_____
_____

2
_____
_____

3
_____
_____

4
_____
_____

5
_____
_____

6
_____
_____

369 METHOD - DAY ☐ of ☐

EVENING GOAL/DESIRED ACTION (COMPLETE)   TIME _____:_____ PM

1.

2.

3.

4.

5.

6.

7.

8.

9.

I RELEASE MY INTENTION WITH GRATITUDE AND LOVE,

DATE ___/___/___ **369 METHOD - DAY** ☐ of ☐

MORNING AFFIRMATION (INITIATE) TIME ___:___ AM

1 _____
_____

2 _____
_____

3 _____
_____

AFTERNOON INTENTION (AMPLIFY) TIME ___:___ PM

1 _____
_____

2 _____
_____

3 _____
_____

4 _____
_____

5 _____
_____

6 _____
_____

369 METHOD - DAY ☐ of ☐

EVENING GOAL/DESIRED ACTION (COMPLETE)　　　　TIME ____:____ PM

1

2

3

4

5

6

7

8

9

I RELEASE MY INTENTION WITH GRATITUDE AND LOVE,

DATE ____/____/____   **369 METHOD - DAY** ☐ of ☐

MORNING AFFIRMATION (INITIATE)   TIME ____:____ AM

1

2

3

AFTERNOON INTENTION (AMPLIFY)   TIME ____:____ PM

1

2

3

4

5

6

MORNING AFFIRMATION (INITIATE)

369 METHOD - DAY ☐ of ☐

EVENING GOAL/DESIRED ACTION (COMPLETE) TIME ____:____ PM

1

2

3

4

5

6

7

8

9

I RELEASE MY INTENTION WITH GRATITUDE AND LOVE,

DATE ____/____/____   **369 METHOD - DAY** ☐ of ☐

MORNING AFFIRMATION (INITIATE)   TIME ____:____ AM

1

2

3

AFTERNOON INTENTION (AMPLIFY)   TIME ____:____ PM

1

2

3

4

5

6

369 METHOD - DAY ☐ of ☐

EVENING GOAL/DESIRED ACTION (COMPLETE)   TIME ____:____ PM

1

2

3

4

5

6

7

8

9

I RELEASE MY INTENTION WITH GRATITUDE AND LOVE,

DATE ____/____/____   **369 METHOD - DAY** ☐ of ☐

MORNING AFFIRMATION (INITIATE)　　　　　　TIME ____:____ AM

1

2

3

AFTERNOON INTENTION (AMPLIFY)　　　　　　TIME ____:____ PM

1

2

3

4

5

6

MORNING AFFIRMATION (INITIATE)

1

369 METHOD - DAY ☐ of ☐

EVENING GOAL/DESIRED ACTION (COMPLETE)   TIME ____:____ PM

1
2
3
4
5
6
7
8
9

I RELEASE MY INTENTION WITH GRATITUDE AND LOVE,

DATE ____/____/____   **369 METHOD - DAY** ☐ of ☐

MORNING AFFIRMATION (INITIATE)   TIME ____:____ AM

1

2

3

AFTERNOON INTENTION (AMPLIFY)   TIME ____:____ PM

1

2

3

4

5

6

369 METHOD - DAY ☐ of ☐

EVENING GOAL/DESIRED ACTION (COMPLETE)　　　　TIME ____:____ PM

1

2

3

4

5

6

7

8

9

I RELEASE MY INTENTION WITH GRATITUDE AND LOVE,

DATE ____/____/____ **369 METHOD - DAY** ☐ of ☐

MORNING AFFIRMATION (INITIATE) TIME ____:____ AM

1

2

3

AFTERNOON INTENTION (AMPLIFY) TIME ____:____ PM

1

2

3

4

5

6

MORNING AFFIRMATION (INITIATE) TIME ____:____ AM

369 METHOD - DAY ☐ of ☐

EVENING GOAL/DESIRED ACTION (COMPLETE)   TIME ____ : ____ PM

1

2

3

4

5

6

7

8

9

I RELEASE MY INTENTION WITH GRATITUDE AND LOVE,

DATE ____/____/____ **369 METHOD - DAY** ☐ of ☐

MORNING AFFIRMATION (INITIATE) TIME ____:____ AM

1

2

3

AFTERNOON INTENTION (AMPLIFY) TIME ____:____ PM

1

2

3

4

5

6

369 METHOD - DAY ☐ of ☐

EVENING GOAL/DESIRED ACTION (COMPLETE)

TIME ____:____ PM

1

2

3

4

5

6

7

8

9

I RELEASE MY INTENTION WITH GRATITUDE AND LOVE,

DATE ____/____/____ **369 METHOD - DAY** ☐ of ☐

MORNING AFFIRMATION (INITIATE)   TIME ____:____ AM

1.

2.

3.

AFTERNOON INTENTION (AMPLIFY)   TIME ____:____ PM

1.

2.

3.

4.

5.

6.

369 METHOD - DAY ☐ of ☐

EVENING GOAL/DESIRED ACTION (COMPLETE)　　　　　TIME ____:____ PM

1.

2.

3.

4.

5.

6.

7.

8.

9.

I RELEASE MY INTENTION WITH GRATITUDE AND LOVE,

DATE ____/____/____   **369 METHOD - DAY** ☐ of ☐

MORNING AFFIRMATION (INITIATE)   TIME ____:____ AM

1

2

3

AFTERNOON INTENTION (AMPLIFY)   TIME ____:____ PM

1

2

3

4

5

6

369 METHOD - DAY ☐ of ☐

EVENING GOAL/DESIRED ACTION (COMPLETE)　　　TIME ____:____ PM

1

2

3

4

5

6

7

8

9

I RELEASE MY INTENTION WITH GRATITUDE AND LOVE,

DATE ____/____/____   **369 METHOD - DAY** ☐ of ☐

MORNING AFFIRMATION (INITIATE)   TIME ____:____ AM

1
_____
_____
_____

2
_____
_____
_____

3
_____
_____
_____

AFTERNOON INTENTION (AMPLIFY)   TIME ____:____ PM

1
_____
_____
_____

2
_____
_____
_____

3
_____
_____

4
_____
_____

5
_____
_____

6
_____
_____

369 METHOD - DAY ☐ of ☐

EVENING GOAL/DESIRED ACTION (COMPLETE)   TIME ____:____ PM

1

2

3

4

5

6

7

8

9

I RELEASE MY INTENTION WITH GRATITUDE AND LOVE,

`3-6-9 METHOD COMPLETED ON`   DATE ____/____/____   TIME ____:____ AM / PM

MANIFESTED INTENTION:

(REWRITE THE EXACT SAME manifestation intention from your 369 exercise)

MANIFESTATION SUCCESS STORY

Use this area to write, illustrate or attach photos, receipts, evidence or proof of your 369 Success Story. This will help to document your manifesting journey and minimize resistence to future manifestations and the Law of Attraction.

`3-6-9 MANIFESTATION COMPLETION`

3-6-9 METHOD COMPLETED ON DATE ___/___/___ TIME ___:___ AM/PM

MANIFESTED INTENTION:

(REWRITE THE EXACT SAME manifestation intention from your 369 exercise)

MANIFESTATION SUCCESS STORY

Use this area to write, illustrate or attach photos, receipts, evidence or proof of your 369 Success Story. This will help to document your manifesting journey and minimize resistence to future manifestations and the Law of Attraction.

3-6-9 MANIFESTATION COMPLETION

3-6-9 METHOD COMPLETED ON   DATE ____/____/____   TIME ____:____ AM/PM

MANIFESTED INTENTION:

(REWRITE THE EXACT SAME manifestation intention from your 369 exercise)

MANIFESTATION SUCCESS STORY

Use this area to write, illustrate or attach photos, receipts, evidence or proof of your 369 Success Story. This will help to document your manifesting journey and minimize resistance to future manifestations and the Law of Attraction.

3-6-9 MANIFESTATION COMPLETION

3-6-9 METHOD COMPLETED ON DATE ___/___/___ TIME ___:___ AM/PM

MANIFESTED INTENTION:

(REWRITE THE EXACT SAME manifestation intention from your 369 exercise)

MANIFESTATION SUCCESS STORY

Use this area to write, illustrate or attach photos, receipts, evidence or proof of your 369 Success Story. This will help to document your manifesting journey and minimize resistance to future manifestations and the Law of Attraction.

3-6-9 MANIFESTATION COMPLETION

3-6-9 METHOD COMPLETED ON   DATE ___/___/___   TIME ___:___ AM/PM

MANIFESTED INTENTION:

(REWRITE THE EXACT SAME manifestation intention from your 369 exercise)

MANIFESTATION SUCCESS STORY

Use this area to write, illustrate or attach photos, receipts, evidence or proof of your 369 Success Story. This will help to document your manifesting journey and minimize resistence to future manifestations and the Law of Attraction.

3-6-9 MANIFESTATION COMPLETION

3-6-9 METHOD COMPLETED ON   DATE ___/___/___   TIME ___:___ AM/PM

MANIFESTED INTENTION:

(REWRITE THE EXACT SAME manifestation intention from your 369 exercise)

MANIFESTATION SUCCESS STORY

Use this area to write, illustrate or attach photos, receipts, evidence or proof of your 369 Success Story. This will help to document your manifesting journey and minimize resistance to future manifestations and the Law of Attraction.

3-6-9 MANIFESTATION COMPLETION

Made in the USA
Monee, IL
05 March 2023